SONG OF THE SONGS OF SOLOMON

SONG OF THE SONGS OF SOLOMON
A NEW VERSION

LAURANCE WIEDER

ACKNOWLEDGMENTS

For this version of Canticles/The Song of Songs, I am (again) indebted to my friend and collaborator Blaire French, who meticulously measured my English against the Hebrew original. Variations on the theme are mine alone.

Copyright © 2020
Laurance Wieder
All rights reserved

**HIGH
LAND
BOOKS**

ISBN: 978-1-7330907-4-2

COVER DESIGN: Matthew Morse/ heymatthew.com

A WORD ABOUT KING SOLOMON

On no one's authority, I think of Ecclesiastes as Solomon's declaration of youthful disenchantment and high ambition. His Proverbs are a handbook of practical criticism for the middle-aged administrator. His love poem, "Song of the Songs of Solomon," is the work of an old poet—in this instance an old man—and an epic of nostalgia.

There's little reason to believe that Solomon son of David is actually the author, or even a subject, of the Song of Songs. Its Hebrew title is "A Song of the Songs: that of Solomon." The Book of Psalms is named for Israel's sweet singer, though only some of the psalms are of King David.

A dramatic cantata, this Song of Songs speaks in three distinct voices—none of them royal. King Solomon appears in allusion, as the proverbial man of wealth and power. But the splendors of his state pale before the singers, who are rich in youth, free in action, and powerful in love.

–L.W.

SONG OF THE SONGS OF SOLOMON

I

She:

> Let him kiss me with kisses of his mouth.
>> Your touch is better than wine;
> your love's scent an oil so sovereign
>> your name is an ointment.
> That's why the young women want you.

Chorus:

> Lead me off with you.
>> Hurry.
> The king carried me into his chamber.
> We tremble and rejoice in you,
>> remember your touch better than wine.
>>> As one, we would taste you.

She:

    I am black, and lovely—
        you daughters of Jerusalem—
    like the bedouins' dark tents,
        like peace behind drawn curtains.
    Don't stare because I'm dark.
        The sun has burnished me.
    My mother's sons glared at me.
        They made me the vineyard keeper—
            my own vineyard I have not kept.
    Tell me now, my soul's beloved:
        where do you graze your ewes?
            how do you rest at noon?
    Need I wrap myself in a shawl
        to seek among your brothers' flocks?

He:

    If you really don't know—
        you fairest among women—

> then track their flocks
>> and feed your kids
>>> outside the shepherds' camp.
> Like a mare in Pharaoh's stable,
>> you are my darling:
> your cheeks adorned with bangles,
>> your neck in ropes of pearls.
> We'll roll gold bangles for you,
>> thread strings of silver beads.

She:

> So long as my king leans on his table,
>> my muskroot gives off scent.
> My love's scent is myrrh to me—
>> he spends all night between my breasts.
> My love's grapes cluster—a whole village to me
>> in the vineyards of Ein Gedi.

He:

    How beautiful, my love,

        How beautiful.

            Your eyes are doves.

She:

    See—you are beautiful my love,

        sweet, even—

        even our bed is green.

He:

    The rafters of our house are cedars,

        our roofbeams cypresses.

She:

    I am a rose of Sharon, a lily of the valley.

He:

    Like a lily in the brambles,

        so my love among the daughters.

She:

    Like a plum tree in the wildwood,

        so my beloved among the sons.

I sat down in his shade with delight,
>   and his fruit tasted sweet.
He brought me to the wine house,
>   and spread love's banner over me.

Refresh me with raisin cakes,
>   sustain me with stone fruits.
Sure, I am sick with love:
>   his left hand beneath my head,
>   his right hand clasps me.

Swear to me,
>   you daughters of Jerusalem—
>   by the wild bucks and does—
if aroused, do not roust
>   out love amid our pleasure.

❧

❧ 2

She:

A voice! My beloved!
> Look, here he comes
>> leaping over the mountains,
>> skipping over the hills.

My love in splendor's like a buck,
> an antlered stag.

See, there he stands, behind our wall.
> He stares through the peekhole.
> He peeps through the lattice.

My love sang and said to me:

"Rise up, you, my love,
> my beautiful you, come away.

For look, the winter's past,
> the rains over, gone.

Flowers bloom on the earth.
The psalm time's upon us
    and the doves' call is heard in our land.
The fig, the green fig ripens
    and grapevines' first buds
        whisper scent.

"Arise, come, my love, my beauty,
    come away.
My pigeon in the rocks' cleft,
    tucked away in the steep—
        show your face.
Let me hear your voice—
    your voice is sweet and
        your face, beautiful.
Let's chase the foxes—
        little foxes—
they spoil our vineyards,
    our vines' tender grape."

My beloved is mine and I am his
    to browse among the lilies
until day breaks and shadows fly.
    My love, turn away like a buck
or an antlered stag
    upon the mountain hollows.

Nights on my bed I desired him,
    my soul's beloved.
I sought him, but he was not found.
I will rise now and walk about the city.
In the streets and in the plazas
    I will seek my soul's beloved.

I sought, but did not find him.
The night watch who patrol the city
    found me.
    "My soul's beloved: have you seen him?"

I'd hardly left them,
> when I found my soul's beloved
> > and I would not let him go
until I brought him to my mother's house,
into the inmost room, where she conceived me.

Swear to me,
> you daughters of Jerusalem,
> > by the wild bucks and does:
if aroused, do not roust
> out love amid our pleasure.

※

🍂 3

Chorus:
> Who is this rising from the wilderness
> > like columns of smoke,
> perfumed with myrrh and frankincense,
> > strewing spice merchants' powders?

> > Look:
> Solomon's litter,
> > picketed by sixty champions
> > > from the mighty men of Israel.
> > Each one wields a sword.
> Each, expert in battle, straps his sword
> > on his thigh
> > against the nights' terrors.

King Solomon made himself a palanquin
>of trees from Lebanon.
He made the uprights silver,
>its poles gold;
inside, purple cushions lovingly embroidered
>by the daughters of Jerusalem.

Come out now, Zion's daughters
and gaze upon the crowned King Solomon,
>the crown his mother placed upon him
>>on the day of his espousal,
>on the day his heart knew joy.

❦ 4

He:
> If you are beautiful, my love....
>> See, you are beautiful:
> your doves' eyes behind your veil;
> your hair tossed like a flock of kids
>> bouncing down Mount Gilead;
> your teeth a flock of shorn ewes
>> come up from the dip,
>>> all matching, none missing.
> Like scarlet thread, your lips
>> and mouth, desirable
> like pomegranate slices, your cheeks
>> behind your veil.
> Your slender neck,
>> like a tower David built
> (a thousand shields hung on it,

all armor for his mighty men);
your two breasts like two fawns,
    a doe's twins
        browsing in the lilies.
Until day breaks and shadows fly
I traverse the mountain of myrrh
    down to the hill of frankincense:
All beautiful, you, my love without flaw.

Come from Lebanon, my bride, come close.
Look out from the white mountains,
    from Amana's feeders,
    from the snowy peak of Mount Hermon,
    from lions' dens, from the leopards' hills.
You ravish my heart, my sister, my bride,
    my heart–rapt through one of your eyes,
    by one link from your necklace.

How beautiful my love, my sister, my bride:
>   your touch, how much better than wine?
>   your fragrance, surpassing all spices.
Your lips drip honeycomb, my bride,
>   milk and honey flow under your tongue,
>   your mantle's scent like Lebanon.

A walled garden my sister, my bride
>   a locked spring, a sealed well:
your limbs a paradise of pomegranate trees
>   with precious fruit,
of henna spiked with nard and saffron,
>   sweet flag and cinnamon,
with every tree of frankincense, of myrrh
>   and aloes, all the choicest spices;
your garden's fountain fed
>   by a well of living waters
and streams from snow-capped mountains.

She:

> Awake, north wind, come to the south.
>> Fan my garden so its perfumes flow.
>
> Let my beloved come into his garden
>> and eat its pleasant fruit.

He:

> I come into my garden, my sister, my bride.
>> I pluck myrrh with my spice.
>
> I eat up my comb with honey.
>> I drink wine with my milk.

Chorus:

> Eat, my loves;
>> drink deep, beloveds.

She:

> I sleep, but my heart wakes:
>> my beloved's voice knocks:

He:

> Open to me, my sister,
>> my dove, my perfect one.

My head crowned with dew,
> my hair drips night mist.

She:
> I stripped off my robe;
>> how do I put it on?
> I washed my feet;
>> how do I soil them?

> My beloved put his hand into the cave;
>> my inwards moaned for him.
> I rose to open to my beloved.
>> My hands oozed myrrh,
> my fingers dripping sweet myrrh
>> on the bolt handle.

❦

❦ 5

She:
>I opened to my beloved,
>>but my beloved turned away: gone.
>
>>My soul left me as he spoke.
>
>I sought him but I did not find him.
>>I called out to him, but no answer.
>
>The night watch who patrol the city
>>found me.
>
>They beat me, bruised me,
>>snatched my veil—
>
>those watchers of the walls.

>Swear to me,
>>you daughters of Jerusalem:
>
>if you find my beloved, do not tell
>>how I am sick with love.

Chorus:

> How is your beloved more beloved,
>> you fairest among women?
> How is your beloved more beloved,
>> that we must swear an oath?

She:

> My beloved, bright and rosy
>> stands out among thousands.
> His head, pure gold,
>> his wavy locks black as a raven;
> his eyes—like doves beside a river bed—
>> bathed in milk, set in gold sockets;
> his cheeks like a spice bed,
>> perfumed towers;
> his two lips, lilies
>> telling promises of myrrh;
> his folding arms, gold inlaid with beryl;

his member polished ivory
    streaked with lapis lazuli;
his legs, marble pillars
    set on pure gold pedestals;
his shape, distinguished,
    like cedars of Lebanon;
his mouth the sweetest
    of all desired things.
This my beloved, this my lover,
    daughters of Jerusalem.

✣

6

Chorus:

> Where has your love gone,
>> you fairest among women?
> Where did your love turn back?
>> We will seek him with you.

She:

> My beloved has gone into his garden,
>> down to the spice beds,
> to graze in the gardens,
>> to gather up lilies.
> I am my beloved's, my beloved is mine:
>> he pastures in the lilies.

He:

> You are fair, my love,
>> like the daughter named Delight,

beautiful as Jerusalem,
        as awesome, as exalted.
Turn your eyes away from me—
    they rattle me:
your hair tossed like a herd of goats
      capering down rocky Gilead;
your teeth a flock of shorn ewes
      come up from the dip,
          all matching, none missing;
your cheeks like pomegranate slices
      seen behind your veil.

Of sixty queens
    and eighty concubines
        and virgins without number—
only she, my dove, my perfect one,
    she, her mother's only one,
        the favorite of she who bore her.

The daughters looked, and call her blessed.
Queens and concubines sing her praises:
"Who is this pearl like the first light,
    fair as the pale moon,
        pure as hot sun,
    awesome as one exalted?"

She:
    I went down into the garden
        where the nut trees grow,
    to look at the green dates,
  to see the grapevine budded,
    the pomegranates bloom.
  I did not know my soul set me
    above the highborn's chariots.

❧ 7

Chorus:

> Return, return, you perfect one.
> Return, return so we may gaze upon you.

He:

> How would you watch the perfect one?
> > like a dance troupe's two-step?
> How beautiful your sandals' footsteps,
> > noble daughter.
> Your ankles, knees, and hips like ornaments
> > made by the master's hand:
> your navel the round bowl
> > of mixed wine, never empty;
> your belly, threshed wheat
> > hemmed in by lilies;

your breasts two fawns,
   a doe's twins;
your neck an ivory tower;
your eyes, pools in the stronghold
   at the common daughters' gate;
your nose, like a white peak
   facing Damascus;
your head you carry like a mountain garden;
   your hair curls purple—
   a king's chained in those locks.
How beautiful and how sweet,
   love, you daughter of delights.
Now you stand straight like a palm tree,
   with your breasts the date clusters.
I thought, "I will climb the palm,
   seize its fruit on the stalk."
Let your breasts be like the vine's clusters
   and your nose scent of apples

and your mouth like fine wine
> that goes down for my beloved,
>> smooth and sweetly,
> sliding through sleepy lips.

She:
> I am my beloved's, and he desires me.
>> Come, my beloved.
> Let's take off to the fields,
>> spend our night in the country.
> We'll see if the vines bud
>> or the grapes blossom
>>> and pomegranates bloom.
> There I'll give you my love:
>> fragrant mandrakes at the entrance and
>> all pleasant fruits, fresh and preserved,
> which I have treasured up, my love, for you.

If only you were like a brother to me,
>   suckled at my mother's breast,
I could meet you in the street, and kiss you.
>   No one would insult me.
I would take your hand and guide you
>   deep inside my mother's house.
>   > She would teach me.
I would pour you drinks—spiced wine,
>   and my pressed pomegranate juice.
His left hand beneath my head,
>   his right hand clasps me.

Swear to me,
>   you daughters of Jerusalem—
>   > by the wild bucks and does—
if aroused, do not roust
>   out love amid our pleasure.

8

Chorus:

> Who is this, come up from the wilderness,
> > leaning on her beloved?

She:

> Under the apple tree, I roused you:
> > there your mother labored with you,
> > > there she writhed and bore you.
> Set me as a seal on your heart,
> > as a seal on your arm,
> for love is fierce as death,
> > jealousy cruel as the grave:
> Its fever fire flashes
> > scorch the altar.
> Mighty waters cannot quench love,
> > nor rivers wash it out.

Should one offer all his family's wealth for love,
>   he scorns contempt.

Chorus:
> We have a little sister
>   and she has no breasts.
> What shall we do for our sister
>   on the day she's spoken for?
> If she is walled,
>   we'll build a silver turret on it;
> and if she be a swinging door,
>   we'll close her in with cedar boards.

She:
> I am a wall, but my breasts are like towers,
>   so I've become one who finds
>   favor in your eyes.

He:

>Solomon, lord of abundance, had a vineyard.
>
>He let the vineyard out to keepers.
>
>Each brought in for his crop
>>a thousand silver pieces.
>
>My vineyard, my own, is before me.
>>Take your thousands, Solomon,
>
>and those two hundred keepers of its fruit.
>>You who dwell in gardens—
>
>attended by companions—
>>let me hear your call.

She:

>Bolt, my beloved.
>>Make like a gazelle
>
>or buck or antlered stag
>>on the mountain of spices.

❧

ALSO BY LAURANCE WIEDER:

from Highland Books:
After Adam: The Books of Moses
Isaiah's Closing Arguments: A New Translation
Words to God's Music: A New Book of Psalms
A Look Ahead: Selected Poems 1966-2018
Poetry History Music Art: Essays 1996-2017

from Oxford:
Chapters Into Verse: Poetry in English Inspired by the Bible
The Poets' Book of Psalms

from Abrams:
King Solomon's Garden: Poems and Art Inspired by the Old Testament

www.ingramcontent.com/pod-product-compliance
Lightning Source LLC
Chambersburg PA
CBHW021134080526
44587CB00012B/1289